EVERYMAN & THE POLE DANCERS

Final episode of an impossible theatrical soap opera—in four quarters

LECH MACKIEWICZ

Currency Press,
Sydney

CURRENT THEATRE SERIES

First published in 2014
by Currency Press Pty Ltd,
PO Box 2287, Strawberry Hills, NSW, 2012, Australia
enquiries@currency.com.au
www.currency.com.au

in association with Auto Da Fe Theatre.

Cataloguing-in-publication data for this title is available from the National Library of Australia website: www.nla.gov.au

Typeset by Dean Nottle for Currency Press.
Printed by SOS Print + Media, Alexandria.
Front cover shows, from left, Kathleen Doyle, Matt Crosby, Jane Bayly and Maude Davey. (Photo: © Adam Hanuszkiewicz).
Cover design by Katy Wall for Currency Press.

Contents

'We've been waiting for the end of the world since
the very beginning,
Even since before we knew how to write.'

Henryk Wrożyński

Everyman & the Pole Dancers was first produced by Auto Da Fe Theatre at the Metanoia Theatre at the Mechanics Institute as part of the Melbourne Fringe Festival, with the following cast:

EVERYMAN	Maude Davey
THE GRANDMOTHER	Jane Bayly
THE GRANDFATHER	Matt Crosby
THE MOTHER	Kathleen Doyle
THE FATHER	Kazuto Shimamoto
THE DAUGHTER	Keina Denda
THE SON	Reece Vella

Writer, director, Lech Mackiewicz
Coproducer, Matt Crosby
Visual installation artist, Naomi Ota
Composer, Noriko Tadano
Lighting designer, Shane Grant
Production manager, Lara Week
Stage manager, Carly McGregor

CHARACTERS

GRANDFATHER: Old, but young at heart. Very physical, proud, but shy at times. He is a theatrical 'animal'. He can be fat or skinny, but he cannot be average in his appearance. Dressed in a tight-fitting costume of a superhero of his dreams. A tall man if Grandmother is short, but a short man if the actor playing Grandmother is tall.

GRANDMOTHER: Old, but (again) young at heart. Dynamic, a born leader. Heavy aggressive make-up. Gypsy-like. There is a strong touch of ethnic-inspired eccentricity to her clothing. She must be either much taller or much shorter than Grandfather.

MOTHER: A beautiful mature woman. Femme fatale, facing her very early retirement. Strong.

FATHER: A handsome man. Film noir gangster appearance with a very delicate inside. Wearing an apron at times to complement his stylish, old-fashioned suit.

DAUGHTER: Spiritual being. Wearing a hood and a tutu. Like all those girls who go to ballet classes and dream of becoming prima ballerinas.

SON: Obsessively pedantic and stuttering at times. A sensible young figure wearing a white tunic over his school uniform. Like an altar boy serving a Catholic mass. His stutter disappears during his solo piece.

EVERYMAN appearing as:

JUDGE/NURSE/SOCIAL WORKER/POLICEMAN/PROSTITUTE/PRIEST/PSYCHIATRIST and as himself.

Everyman is ageless and sexless. Alternatively Everyman is 1,000 years old (young?), male, with a rather sleazy kind of personal charm and charisma, who enjoys taking on girlish mannerisms and accessories for a scene or two. He runs this show. He is everyone and no-one at the same time.

WARM-UP/PROLOGUE

Curtains drawn.

EVERYMAN *enters as* EVERYMAN.

He lights a cigar. He smokes as he speaks.

EVERYMAN: [*as himself*] The End is looming. It is coming soon. The volcanoes of the Island of Volcanoes have awoken and begun spitting out dark clouds of ashes, veiling the skies of the world. The great underwater worlds of the oceans have awoken and begun their ascent to the surface, forcing vast masses of water to rise and flood the continents. Communication has stopped. The only hope is in redemption. But redemption will not save the human family of today. Redemption will only mark a direction for future cultures, those which will subsequently populate this world. For the time being, all that is known is this simple truth: The civilisations of today are doomed to follow the great civilisations of the past into the dark eye of destruction, for their worth is nothing. The gods are not crazy. The gods have waited patiently. The time will come, in a distant future, that the gods grant this world a new race of inhabitants. We must learn for them. Now, in the last moments before the final fall, it is our time for the reconstruction. We have danced freely from Pole to Pole, from one end of the world to the other, using all its wealth and goodness, with disregard for the highest laws of divine nature. The whole of the world is our crime scene. This is an attempt to reconstruct the murder of our life as we knew it. We were family once…

Pause.

By the time this cigar is finished our story will be over.

He places the cigar on an ashtray standing on the left side of the stage. The cigar will stay there, burning away slowly.

All the world is a stage. And since we are on television… this is a soap opera: Camera? Set! And: Action!

EVERYMAN *exits, opening the curtains.*

OPENING QUARTER

In the dark, a piercing whistle can be heard. Lights.

EVERYMAN *enters as* POLICEMAN.

He crosses the stage.

He goes past GRANDFATHER *and* GRANDMOTHER, *chained to the lamppost.*

He exits.

GRANDMOTHER: [*reading a statement*] 'We, Grandmother (that's me) and Grandfather (that's him)—we (I and he)… in short: *we* declare ourselves officially…' Hm? Why officially?

GRANDFATHER *groans like a lion.*

Okay, okay, okay… 'We declare ourselves officially unfit for retirement village accommodation. We declare ourselves unwilling to be subject to any retirement village activities. We state hereby that we don't want to mix with our likes, namely: any other grandmothers and grandfathers—those repulsive, far-beyond-their-use-by-date old farts!'

EVERYMAN *enters as* SOCIAL WORKER.

EVERYMAN/SOCIAL WORKER: What about great-grandmothers? [*Pause.*] And great-grandfathers?

GRANDFATHER *roars like a lion.*

GRANDMOTHER: What about them?

EVERYMAN/SOCIAL WORKER: They are not your likes. They are older, therefore wiser; therefore you can learn something from them.

GRANDMOTHER: Give us examples. Like what?

EVERYMAN: Like: life without food, fun without fun, life without alcohol, how to breath with a respirator, life without light, life without sex…

GRANDFATHER *roars like a lion.*

GRANDMOTHER: What is your problem, now? Let the man finish his litany. He hasn't scored a single point, so far. [*To* SOCIAL WORKER]We learned how to live without sex a long time ago, by ourselves. No need for assistance.

GRANDFATHER *roars like a lion.*

EVERYMAN: Is sex the issue, then? We can provide occasional sex services by means of our highly qualified Nurstitute. Our Nurstitutes can engage in a wide range of sexual services, with those in need under extreme duress, while at the same time performing a basic cardiopulmonary resuscitation. Let me explain: commonly known as CPR—it is an emergency procedure performed in an effort to manually preserve intact brain function and to restore spontaneous blood circulation and breathing in a person experiencing cardiac arrest, which, let me lay it out openly, is more than likely to happen to a person aged eighty-five-plus nearing a climax. Such a person often becomes unresponsive with no breathing… or abnormal breathing.

GRANDMOTHER: I told you!

GRANDFATHER *roars like a lion.*

Okay, okay, okay. You can carry on. Convince me, baby boy, because … I'm not convinced at all.

EVERYMAN/SOCIAL WORKER: 'A standard CPR procedure involves chest compressions… yes, read my lips: at least five centimetres deep and… yes, you are not mistaken: at a rate of at least one hundred per minute, in an effort to create artificial circulation by manually pumping blood through the heart. In addition, the rescuer provides breaths, by exhaling into the subject's mouth, which is more than convenient during the intercourse, with kissing included, which in turn may be more expensive, but what the hell! [*Pause.*] It may be performed both in and outside of a retirement compound.'

MOTHER *enters.*

MOTHER: Do you provide home visits?

EVERYMAN *puts on a wig and becomes* EVERYMAN/PROSTITUTE.

EVERYMAN/PROSTITUTE: It will cost you more.

MOTHER: How much?

EVERYMAN/PROSTITUTE: Twice as much.

MOTHER: I told you!

FATHER *enters.*

FATHER: Can we negotiate the price?

EVERYMAN/PROSTITUTE: You can join our loyalty program.

FATHER: What do you mean?

EVERYMAN/PROSTITUTE: Once you've used our services ten times, you get a free… you know… service.

FATHER: Do I?

MOTHER: We'd prefer a discount. It's not for him. It's for the grandparents. They might not pull through ten services. And then, what?

FATHER: We can take over, can't we?

EVERYMAN/PROSTITUTE: Actually, I'm not sure how it works. I think it is linked to the person, like car insurance.

FATHER: Car insurance is linked to a car not to a person, right?

EVERYMAN/PROSTITUTE: That's what I mean: Our loyalty card is linked to a person like car insurance is linked to a car!

GRANDMOTHER: They treat us like cars! Can you imagine that?

GRANDFATHER *cannot imagine that.*

MOTHER: Oh, shut up, Grandma! [*Turning to* EVERYMAN] We'll be interested in your offer when you come up with a better… offer. Not a loyalty card but a discount. Your service seems very desirable these days, I myself can sense a little tickling sensation in my private parts, but I cannot digest the pricing. Wow! Thank you for your trouble. I will be in touch.

EVERYMAN/PROSTITUTE: I understand. Go fuck yourselves, losers!

EVERYMAN *takes the wig off.*

EVERYMAN *exits.*

MOTHER: If I only could…

FATHER: You can if you try really hard. No pain, no gain.

EVERYMAN *returns briefly.*

EVERYMAN: Here is my number. On call 24/7.

EVERYMAN *exits.*

MOTHER: A loyalty card! A rewards card! A points card! A club card! It is just a piece of plastic. Visually it is similar to a credit card. It identifies the cardholder as a member of a loyalty program. Loyalty cards are part of a bigger system. I hate loyalty cards! They are there to make sure that you remain faithful to just one brand name.

FATHER: It sounds like our marriage!

MOTHER: Exactly!

FATHER: Did I ever get a marriage loyalty card?

MOTHER: And did I? I am a free man!

FATHER: Woman, maybe?

MOTHER: Man! I am making a large-scale statement here! I am a free man and I don't tolerate any opposition to my will. To top it all with some icing I have another statement coming shortly. But firstly…

FATHER: You are like your mother.

GRANDFATHER: She is!

GRANDMOTHER: I told you, I am your man.

GRANDFATHER: You have balls, I know.

MOTHER: That's my point. But firstly… But firstly… I forgot…

EVERYMAN *enters briefly.*

EVERYMAN: The loyalty cards!

MOTHER: The loyalty cards. Thank you! [*Pause.*] The loyalty cards can be used to determine any given customer's favourite brand of beer, for example, or whether that customer is a vegetarian or not, or a vegan or not, or a lesbian…

GRANDMOTHER: Where did you learn all that?

MOTHER: Not at school and not from you! This kind of knowledge comes from self-education. And now, the statement: I am a *gay* man!

MOTHER *exits.*

GRANDMOTHER: She doesn't know what she's talking about.

FATHER: She always knows what she's talking about. And you? You ruined our family life, so if I were you, I'd say no more.

FATHER *exits.*

GRANDMOTHER: That's my boy.

GRANDFATHER *roars like a lion.*

What?

GRANDFATHER: He is not yours!

GRANDMOTHER *doesn't understand. She starts crying.*

I've been trying to tell you for a long time, but you won't listen! I'm sorry. [*Pause.*] Life is such a bitch… Sometimes.

EVERYMAN *enters briefly (as* EVERYMAN*).*

EVERYMAN: Has anyone called for me?

GRANDMOTHER: What's the time?

EVERYMAN: Quarter past.

GRANDMOTHER: So, no. Not yet. Too early.

EVERYMAN *exits.*

Far too early.

GRANDFATHER: But it will come—you know. Sooner rather than later. And there will be no running away from it. From the past…

GRANDMOTHER: From the future. I meant our future.

GRANDFATHER: From our past. Is the future anything but the deep bruising on my cheek resulting from the past? The future arrives from our past. Without our past there would be no mention of the future. There would be no future!

GRANDMOTHER: Shut up! Without your past we'd be better off, methinks. Let's dance and forget.

GRANDFATHER: We are chained to this… lamppost. Remember?

GRANDMOTHER: I do. Let's dance. We can do what we please. I am a free man.

They dance.

DAUGHTER *and* SON *enter and dance.*

MOTHER *and* FATHER *watch them. Then they join the dance.*

EVERYMAN *(as* POLICEMAN*) enters. He blows his whistle.*

Everyone stops dancing.

EVERYMAN/POLICEMAN: This is an illegal gathering. [*Pause.*] Firstly, I will arrest you all. Then I will issue fines. [*Pause.*] Or I can issue fines first and then arrest those who oppose the enforcement of law. What would you prefer?

SON: This is a legal gathering. I have all the necessary paperwork. Here. The local authorities have licensed it.

EVERYMAN/POLICEMAN: Sorry. My apologies. Sorry. Got the wrong address.

EVERYMAN *exits.*

EVERYMAN *immediately comes back.*

All the same: You two are arrested. Follow me.

MOTHER *and* FATHER *exit following* EVERYMAN.

DAUGHTER: And you two, what have you been up to?

GRANDMOTHER *and* GRANDFATHER *don't know what they've been up to.*

SON: C'mon! The chains, the statements? What's up? We miss you.

GRANDMOTHER: I bet. Who'd love you like I would? Not him.

GRANDFATHER *hisses like a snake.*

SON: Not much time left. We need you.

GRANDMOTHER: How many lovers have you had? A thousand? Two thousand? Three? Were any of them better than I am?

DAUGHTER: Hey, you. What are you talking about? What do you want from him? He's only seven.

SON: Seven and a half.

GRANDFATHER *hisses like a snake.*

GRANDMOTHER: My love for you is unconditional. Platonic. I expect nothing in return. I'd do anything for you. Anything. You understand? I am your grandma! Cooking and washing, singing and dancing… anything—just name it.

SON: We need you in the retirement compound. In the village.

GRANDMOTHER: You cannot have that. We don't belong there.

GRANDFATHER: No, we don't.

GRANDMOTHER: But why?

SON: They'll cut the benefit.

GRANDMOTHER: This is our benefit they will cut. Not your problem.

SON: It is our problem. We live off your benefit. Part of it.

GRANDMOTHER: Then live of somebody else's benefit. Can't see that problem of yours.

SON: Don't you understand?

DAUGHTER: Oh, c'mon! Tell her. Deliver the message! Communicate! Implicate your point!

SON: Alright: I love you too, Grandmother! I adore you. I worship you… what more can I say? I've always loved you.

GRANDMOTHER: You can tell me if you find me irresistible?

GRANDFATHER: Yes: You can tell her that, because I'd like to know, because I do.

SON: I find you uncontrollably overpowering, I do.

GRANDMOTHER: Then get the hell out of my sight, now!

SON *gets out of her sight.*

GRANDMOTHER: And you too, young lady.

DAUGHTER *resists.*

GRANDFATHER *hisses like a snake.*

DAUGHTER *follows* SON. *She gets out of the* GRANDPARENTS*' sight.*

GRANDFATHER: Do you really love him?

GRANDMOTHER: I do, yet I wonder… I may be too old for him, you know. Too much life knowledge may weigh heavily on our relationship in the future?

GRANDFATHER: There will be no future. I know. No future for me. I see darkness.

GRANDMOTHER: Same thing. There is no difference between future and present in relation to too much life experience. Anyway, if not him, then who?… I can give him so much. Introduce him to life in a way no other woman could. Not even his mother. This is true love! Pure, platonic, with no expectations on my end. Without its dirty earthly trappings.

EVERYMAN *enters briefly (as* NURSE*).*

EVERYMAN/NURSE: Anyone for a change?

No answer.

EVERYMAN/NURSE *exits.*

GRANDFATHER: Speaking of which: How are we going to change our nappies here?

GRANDMOTHER: No nappies! It's part of our protest! Good old chamber pot will do. Some human dignity, please!

GRANDFATHER: I've forgotten. Right, dignity, yes…

GRANDMOTHER: You don't have much time left. I want you to give me your permission to…

GRANDFATHER: No! [*Pause.*] Not yet! [*He hisses.*] I had a dream: the Fish Pond Dream. The Fish Pond Theory Dream. And in my dream I saw that little man, that vicious little man, with his vicious big smile, and his tight leather pants and little moustache to complete the picture. And that little man had a big pond: The Fish Pond he called it… *His* Fish Pond he called it, although it wasn't certain, whether he had any rights to claim the Fish Pond as his. As is generally the case in dreams: The ownership rights are never easily established by the outsider—the dreamer.

GRANDMOTHER: You weren't in your dream? An outside dreamer? A dreaming outsider?

GRANDFATHER: Mhm?

GRANDMOTHER: You sure it's not a fairytale of old?

GRANDFATHER: Even if it was, I still dreamt it.

GRANDMOTHER: When?

GRANDFATHER: Just then, it seems. Yesterday… maybe… it all seems to be not so long ago… memories, dreams… yes… the past is haunting me… yes… yesterday, it all happened yesterday.

GRANDMOTHER: Back to your dream, you animal!

GRANDFATHER: [*hissing like a snake*] The Fish Pond Theory Dream.

EVERYMAN *(as* POLICEMAN*) blows his whistle offstage.*

EVERYMAN *enters as* PRIEST.

EVERYMAN/PRIEST: It's time. Would you like to confess?

GRANDMOTHER: What time is it?

EVERYMAN/PRIEST: Quarter past.

GRANDFATHER: Too late! You missed your chance, today, padre. Quarter past. Too late.

EVERYMAN/PRIEST: You missed yours. You can go to hell.

EVERYMAN/PRIEST *exits.*

GRANDFATHER: I know that much.

GRANDMOTHER: And aren't you so bloody right.

GRANDFATHER: Let's dance and forget.

They dance.

MOTHER *and* DAUGHTER *enter and dance.*

SON *and* FATHER *watch them. Then they join in the dance.*

EVERYMAN POLICEMAN *blows his whistle to bring the dance party to an end.*

FATHER *and* SON, DAUGHTER *and* MOTHER *run for cover.*

EVERYMAN/POLICEMAN *follows.*

MOTHER *and* DAUGHTER *return.*

DAUGHTER: Are you serious? A gay man?
MOTHER: Yes. Nothing can be done, I am afraid.
DAUGHTER: You are in love with a gay man?

Pause.

MOTHER: I *am* a gay man. I finally understand myself.
DAUGHTER: Is Father gay, then? Is he, too?
MOTHER: How am I to know? Ask him.
DAUGHTER: Are you gay, Father?

FATHER *enters and crosses the stage.*

FATHER: I am not. Though I always wanted to join a swingers' club.

FATHER *exits.* EVERYMAN/POLICEMAN *crosses the stage following* FATHER.

EVERYMAN/POLICEMAN: You are under arrest!

He exits.

DAUGHTER: He is not gay.
MOTHER: What do I care? I am in love with that gay man.
EVERYMAN: [*as* EVERYMAN, *offstage*] I am gay. I mean, not only gay. But predominantly gay.
MOTHER: And that's the whole, naked truth. I'm leaving. Mother no more, woman no more. Destiny awaits!

SON *enters.*

SON: You cannot, Mother. The family needs you. Mother! [*Pause. Addressing* DAUGHTER] And what about you? Can't you see your mother's suffering? It's all due to the grandma's and grandpa's rebellion. Mum cannot comprehend the whole situation. She starts to distort her reality and in return the reality surrounding her is starting to distort the way she sees reality. She is suffering. And she is becoming obsessed with ideas, which can free her from our circle of life—from our family. She is having obsessive fantasies…

EVERYMAN *enters as* PSYCHOLOGIST.

EVERYMAN/PSYCHOLOGIST: Obsessive fantasies. Intrusive fantasies. Intrusive thoughts. Let me explain: Intrusive thoughts result from unwanted cognitive activities accompanied by worry, distraction, daydreaming, which interfere with our ability to perform, but also, and more importantly, our ability to engage in productive thoughts. Commonly associated with distress, intrusive thoughts are a universal experience. So you shouldn't think yourself unusual. Often, mothers have intrusive, unwanted thoughts after giving birth… Intrusive thoughts… are impossible to escape… as I said: a common experience for mothers, becoming awfully distressing and developing into Obsessive Compulsive Gay Man Disorder (OCGMD). Even though we can name it we don't know its boundaries… its full effects, so to speak. In research to date, the flow of human thought still remains the mystery of mysteries. It is widely accepted, that…

MOTHER: I love you!

EVERYMAN/PSYCHOLOGIST: … we know nothing about ourselves. Fuckin' hell! Don't say? You still have to pay for the visit.

EVERYMAN/PSYCHOLOGIST *exits, followed by* MOTHER.

DAUGHTER: She gave birth to us quite a long time ago.

SON: Yes.

EVERYMAN/PSYCHOLOGIST: [*offstage*] An intrusive thought takes a long time to blossom, sometimes.

SON: Certainly.

DAUGHTER: Now?

FATHER: [*offstage*] You are facing a major crisis, young people. Include me out.

GRANDFATHER *howls.*

GRANDMOTHER: And he's bloody right.

DAUGHTER: Now? What now?!

GRANDMOTHER: Don't yell at him! I love him. You have a few options.

SON: Don't yell at me. Thank you, Grandmother, I love you. We have a few options.

DAUGHTER: Not too many it seems, with Grandpa's past catching up with him we are running out of time.

SON: We can force them to sign statements. [*Pause.*] We can get them diagnosed with some kind of mental disease. [*Pause.*] We can just ignore them. [*Pause.*] We can adopt their respective personalities, adopt their respective physicalities, muster their habits and their speech patterns—in short: *we* become *them*, and…

GRANDMOTHER: And you end up here, my love. At this very lamppost. Dancing madly to our tune…

GRANDFATHER *laughs like a horse.*

DAUGHTER: What do you say to that?

SON: *We* become *them*, and we move to the retirement village, because by adopting their personalities and appearances we don't acquire their will to rebel against their family—against us. One's will is not necessarily linked to one's character. Actors do that—they make decisions based on what they want as actors and not what the characters want. We'll act.

DAUGHTER: I'm not sure. There are many approaches to and definitions of acting. So I hear.

SON: Do you want the lifestyle or do you want to dream of the lifestyle? We either act or we wave bye-bye to our ambitions.

DAUGHTER: And our ambitions are?

GRANDMOTHER: To be able to do nothing but be able to do anything and everything?!

SON: Couldn't phrase it any better. Have I mentioned that I love you, Grandmother?

GRANDMOTHER: You have. So now you can just take her and together you can just get lost! I need some privacy for my solo piece.

They do as told.

GRANDMOTHER*'s solo piece: 'Remember the Royal Visit?'…*

GRANDMOTHER: It was thirty-six years ago. Maybe fifty-six years ago. Our whole family went to the Capital City. We were family, then. Him? Maybe not so much. We stayed in the Grace Hotel. I loved that hotel: fin de siècle meets art deco, high ceilings, glass doors! He watched some comedy on TV. Nothing would make him go for a walk that morning. Not even the visiting Royals on display. Maybe he had a hangover. I took the kids, all four… or three of them? Did we have three then? Maybe. Four maybe? I was wearing the golden dress I had for special occasions. And a shawl he gave me for my birthday. I looked at myself in the mirror and I was proud. He didn't notice. He watched television. And then we went for breakfast. In the hotel's foyer he met a woman… In the foyer. She was older and interesting. She knew all about football. He got spellbound. He spent hours talking to her. He only noticed we weren't back when it was time to leave and he realised things were not packed. I packed our luggage. Always. If he did it we'd need four trunks each. I had a special system… 'system' is a good word… a system for folding and packing clothes. I could fit my wardrobe into my handbag if I wanted. He started panicking. He alerted the staff. He asked the maid… yes, the maid… the bellboy, the concierge, the manager. The manager called the police. And the police arrived. They took photographs of the room as if we were dead or something… never liked police taking photos. Scared me. Such a sight always scared me. They asked him to recreate the morning. He was to walk slowly through everything he did, we did, that morning. A reconstruction, they called it. The reconstruction. He couldn't remember anything. He couldn't remember his family leaving that morning. Then, as he was walking by the press stand, he saw the evening newspaper. We were on the front page. I kept that paper. I have even more press clippings. We became the most famous family for that one day. The Royals stopped when they were passing by in their carriage. The Queen liked my golden dress… and the kids—we had the most beautiful children in the world. They invited us to hop in. 'Hop in', the Queen said. Yes. They took us for a ride. We spent the whole day with the Royals. Like Royals. We were popular that day. An overnight sensation. People would point at us with their fingers and say: 'It's them! The woman in the golden dress and her children.' But he missed it. It felt as if he was dead… He died a week later, anyway. Didn't he?

The end of GRANDMOTHER*'s solo piece.*

Do you remember the royal visit?

GRANDFATHER: It wasn't me. I remember it, alright, but it wasn't me.

GRANDMOTHER: Whatever.

GRANDFATHER: Am I the only fuckin' grandpa on this planet? In your life?

GRANDMOTHER: You are.

GRANDFATHER: But was I? Then?

GRANDMOTHER: Whatever. Fish Pond Dream Theory.

GRANDFATHER: The Fish Pond Theory Dream.

GRANDMOTHER: Whatever. Carry on.

GRANDFATHER: Not 'whatever'. It is crucial! Is there a priest here?

EVERYMAN: [*offstage*] Is this a confession?

GRANDFATHER: [*laughing like a horse*] No. A dream.

EVERYMAN: [*offstage*] Too bad.

EVERYMAN *enters as* PSYCHIATRIST.

GRANDMOTHER: Will you give me permission to…?

GRANDFATHER: Not yet… Little man, that vicious little man… vicious big smile… little moustache… I remember well. And that little man had a big pond: The Fish Pond. It was his idea. You must understand. It was his mad idea, to put as much fish in that little pond as possible. One would think that it was impossible to put more fish in that little pond, yet he would bring more and more fish to make them live in the muddy, airless waters of the pond. Big and small, fat and skinny, red fin and blue fin, rich and poor. The pond made all the fish equal in the eyes of the little man. They were just fish. And he hated fish. Every year the little man made sure the pond was full. Then he would get rid of the fish. He would start by lowering the dam so the water level would fall and the fish would have even less water space to live in. Less and less. Boats would be dropped on the surface of what used to be water but now was a fish pile. And the fish gasping for water regardless of their colour, age, sex or size were picked and thrown into brown crates and transported into an unspecified direction for an unspecified destination, but surely never to be heard of again. The madman laughed, as he hated fish, and he'd allow only the two strongest species to survive in a paddle on the very bottom of the Fish Pond. Then he'd raise the dam again to let the fish breed. And again he'd bring more fish in, all the fish he could find and buy, so as the year neared its end, the little vicious man could repeat his horrific ritual. As it was his plan to erase all the fish from the waters of the world and keep just enough for himself so that he would be able to see some fish die every year.

EVERYMAN/PSYCHIATRIST: That's one hell of a dream you just had. Are you sure you aren't a Pisces?

GRANDFATHER: What?

EVERYMAN/PSYCHIATRIST: Pisces? Star sign. Just a joke. I can't come up with anything more original. I certainly won't eat fish and chips for a while now.

GRANDMOTHER: Don't you understand? It's not a dream, it is his way of dealing with reality. It's his past catching up with him. Where did you get your diploma from, you shrink?

GRANDFATHER: Shut up! I'm not who you think I am. I am not responsible for anything you might insinuate. Not at all. Don't listen to her. She is in love with a younger man. I am not bad. My fault cannot be proven, or else I might die—I am of poor health lately. Don't judge me too fast.

EVERYMAN *puts on a judge's wig.*

EVERYMAN/JUDGE: The time has come. Confess.

MOTHER/DAUGHTER/FATHER: [*offstage*] We all have the right to hear.

EVERYMAN/JUDGE: No. It is his solo piece.

GRANDFATHER: In which case we have to postpone the hearing. I am not ready to face the truth without my family's support.

EVERYMAN/JUDGE: You have no other option but to proceed.

GRANDFATHER: Yes, I do have an-other option. [*He laughs like a horse.*] I choose to die. Right here, right now. I shall be no more!

Opening Quarter ends here.

MID QUARTER

GRANDMOTHER, *chained to a lamppost. On the other side there is a funeral urn chained to the same lamppost.*

GRANDMOTHER: [*sobbing*] How could you do this to me? My protest is kind of pointless now. We were to share an adventurous run of freedom… together.

GRANDFATHER'S VOICE: We still can do it. You just have to take me along, wherever you go.

GRANDMOTHER: Shush. They might hear you. It's worked so far. They might hear you and your plan will fail again. You have come close to the end of your story. You almost revealed yourself.

GRANDFATHER'S VOICE: But that's not my story. I borrowed it to get rid of the problem. To solve the problem. To avoid the compound.

GRANDMOTHER: I know. Yet: what do I know?

GRANDFATHER*'s voice roars like a lion.*

Piercing sound of a whistle.

EVERYMAN *enters as* POLICEMAN.

EVERYMAN/POLICEMAN: Now, we've heard it. You are under arrest. You must confess now.

GRANDFATHER'S VOICE: [*hissing like a snake*] Damn it!

GRANDMOTHER: I told you.

EVERYMAN *takes the urn from* GRANDMOTHER *and places it in the middle.*

EVERYMAN: Everything you say now… from now on… may be, or may be not used against you, so choose your words carefully.

EVERYMAN *puts on a judge's wig.*

EVERYMAN/JUDGE: For training and quality purposes your solo piece may be recorded and used as warning material for future generations of yourselves. Proceed.

GRANDMOTHER: Your Honour. Excuse me. Can we dance before… you know? It can be his… our last move together.

EVERYMAN/JUDGE: It's not exactly in accordance with the protocol, but… Yes, go ahead.

GRANDMOTHER: Thank you, Your Honour. I love saying 'Your Honour', Your Honour. Your Honour doesn't mind, I hope.

EVERYMAN/JUDGE: Nope.

GRANDMOTHER *takes the urn and starts dancing.*

MOTHER, FATHER, DAUGHTER *and* SON *appear and watch.*

GRANDFATHER *also appears. He joins* GRANDMOTHER.

When the dance finishes, GRANDFATHER *disappears.*

All are in tears.

GRANDMOTHER *returns the urn to the centre.*

GRANDMOTHER: You have your family's support, my dear. Be brave.
EVERYMAN/JUDGE: Thank you. Now proceed.

GRANDFATHER*'s solo piece: 'Remember the Army Crossing?'...*

GRANDFATHER'S VOICE: My village, in summer, was a picture of paradise. It was fifty-six, maybe seventy-six years ago. Slow flowing river. Lazy afternoon sun. Birds, cows, even dogs couldn't be bothered to move or to use their voices. Just that vibrating, hot air and the occasional insect, cutting through the space as if not realising that it wasn't the thing to do on a summer afternoon. Peaceful. Peaceful. What a wonderful world. [*Pause.*] The first explosion was deafening! Bang! And then another one: Bang! And another one: Bang! Bang! I don't know how long I lay there, but it was quiet again. Except for a remote ringing sound in my ears. Nothing but the ringing: rrrrrrrrrrr. So I heard nothing, but I saw her lying not so far. She moved her mouth, I think she was saying something. It looked as if she was screaming, but I heard nothing. Not a word. Then she stopped moving. She had her eyes open and kept looking at me. But she was absent. She wasn't there. [*Pause.*] I hate violence. The slightest hint of violence makes me sick. I couldn't stand watching her being beaten and raped by men in uniforms. They were army men. There was a war going on. I knew nothing of it. It wasn't my war, it wasn't my army. But as the last man was forcing himself upon her, in that mute picture I was watching, I screamed. I couldn't hear my scream either. I threw myself at the army man and hit him on the head with a stone. And hit him once more. And again, and again. Until the head felt soft and it turned red. The army man fell on her and she pushed him off. She closed her eyes. I stood there and I couldn't understand what had just happened. She got up and she started to undress me. Then she indicated for me to pull off the uniform of the army man. 'Put it on'—these were the first words I heard. 'Put it on.' I put on the uniform and I became one of them. 'We are the only ones left. We are strong, we can make it.' I could hear, but the ringing tone remained. It stayed. It is still there. I can hear it now. Sometimes I think that animals can hear the ringing too, then they scream with their voices and the ringing goes away. But only for a short while. It always comes back. [*Pause.*] She told me to hit her and to drag her towards the forest, where we could hide. I couldn't hit her. I hate violence. So she hit me and I had to defend myself. I dragged her to the forest. And it was there where she fainted. Maybe she died. No, she fainted. I had to run. She didn't see it when I got caught. No she didn't. The documents they found in one of the pockets of the uniform carried that name you mention, when you accuse me of all those atrocities. But it wasn't my name. It is the name of the man I am not. I killed that man. I know he is guilty of an estimated 25,000 human deaths, he is guilty of bestiality towards other human beings. He raped, he tortured, he found pleasure in cruelty. But I killed that man. I am not that man. I am yet another victim of war. [*Pause.*] I wasn't in the boat catching the fish. I was the fish. Maybe the strongest fish of them all, but one of them. I am a fish, like you. I hate violence. I wish she was there, so she could see it when they caught me, so she could tell them the truth. But she wasn't there. [*He howls like a wolf.*] I accept gladly the sentence you are about to pass on me. I understand that it will be five years in a retirement compound, but due to my poor health and my old age I will be allowed to spend that time in prison, am I right?

EVERYMAN/JUDGE: Five years it is. [*Pause.*] Five years for the second time! [*Pause.*] Five years in prison for the third… and final time! Sold!

EVERYMAN/JUDGE *takes the urn and exits.*

GRANDFATHER *enters. He chains himself to the lamppost.*

GRANDFATHER: Remember the army crossing?

GRANDMOTHER: I do, but I don't remember you.

GRANDFATHER: You don't remember me?

GRANDMOTHER: I do remember you, but I can't remember your story. Maybe it wasn't me.

GRANDFATHER: It wasn't you.

GRANDMOTHER: Then maybe that wasn't you… in your story.

GRANDFATHER: It wasn't me, but it was me at the same time. There were two of me in that story.

GRANDMOTHER: I am confused. I don't understand why five years?

Which one of you? Guilty or not guilty?

EVERYMAN/JUDGE *returns briefly.*

EVERYMAN/JUDGE: Guilty. Or not guilty. What's the difference now? It is a good story, though. Believable, moving… et cetera… So good, in fact, it is impossible to believe. So a five-year sentence sounds just: you got it for the story.

EVERYMAN *exits.*

GRANDMOTHER: But you are dead. You were dead. Just then.

GRANDFATHER: That's right. I reconsidered. Five years in prison is better than being dead. It also solves our problem: prison is not a retirement compound. So I'm back. I won't be in any kind of retirement accommodation.

GRANDMOTHER: It solves your problem. Not our problem. Unless I can go to prison with you. Can I?

EVERYMAN/JUDGE *appears briefly.*

EVERYMAN/JUDGE: Nope!

GRANDMOTHER: There you go. I cannot. I have no other option but to follow your footsteps and be no more.

GRANDFATHER: But I am here now.

GRANDMOTHER: Here now, there tomorrow. You are not to be trusted. Therefore: goodbye and don't cry for me anymore.

Mid Quarter ends here.

THIRD QUARTER

GRANDFATHER, *chained to the lamppost.*

On the other side, Grandmother's urn, chained to the same lamppost.

MOTHER *and* EVERYMAN *as* PSYCHIATRIST.

EVERYMAN/PSYCHIATRIST: One can have too much energy. One can have too much concentration. One can never have too much attention! This is your problem.

MOTHER: I don't have a problem. For the first time in my life I don't have a problem.

EVERYMAN/PSYCHIATRIST: And that's your problem. This is exactly why you lost yourself. You lost your balance. And your attention…

MOTHER: I haven't lost anything.

EVERYMAN/PSYCHIATRIST: Shut the fuck up!

MOTHER: I love you.

EVERYMAN/PSYCHIATRIST: Shut the fuck up! You lost your balance… and… attention brings energy and concentration into balance, in other words it brings equanimity. The balance balances… I mean: attention balances different aspects of the mind. All mental factors depend on attention. And if we have balanced minds—we will have balanced lives.

MOTHER: Together? Can we balance our minds together?

EVERYMAN/PSYCHIATRIST: What?

MOTHER: I can balance you if you balance me a bit.

EVERYMAN/PSYCHIATRIST: It is an individual process. You cannot balance me!

MOTHER: We shall see.

MOTHER *embraces* EVERYMAN/PSYCHIATRIST *and starts dancing.*

FATHER *enters. Followed by* SON.

They watch MOTHER *dance with* EVERYMAN/PSYCHIATRIST.

EVERYMAN/PSYCHIATRIST *runs offstage.* MOTHER *follows.*

FATHER: So it is just the three of us. Three men.

SON: Yes.

GRANDFATHER: Include me out! I am no more.

SON: You were no more but now, you are, Grandfather. Grandmother is no more!

GRANDFATHER: Yes and no. I am and I'm not. I am in prison, technically speaking. I'm no more.

FATHER: There are only two of us then. Technically.

GRANDFATHER: Wait! What about Mother?

FATHER & SON: She is no more. She said so.

GRANDFATHER: What about the young one? Your sister?

SON: My sister? Possibly. But she is no more. She followed Grandmother.

GRANDFATHER: So you don't need us anymore. You don't need our benefit? Our pension? Or do you?

SON: I do.

FATHER: So there are only two or three of us left.

SON: What difference does that make?

FATHER: None, really. Three or two—not much swing left between us, anyway. And we are family…

GRANDFATHER: Include me out.

GRANDMOTHER'S VOICE: You aren't my family anyway.

GRANDFATHER: That's right. I tried to tell you that before. We aren't related.

GRANDMOTHER'S VOICE: Thank God! Otherwise we couldn't get married.

EVERYMAN/PRIEST *enters briefly.*

EVERYMAN/PRIEST: Someone has called for me.

GRANDFATHER: Not you. God.

EVERYMAN/PRIEST: I'm God's rep, here. I represent God.

SON: Which one?

EVERYMAN/PRIEST: Does it matter? Not much time left.

SON & FATHER: Give me a break. Go away!

EVERYMAN/PRIEST *goes.*

FATHER: Two or three of us left.

SON: Can we get one thing straight: he was right. Not much time left. We need your benefit. And now we can't have your benefit since Grandmother is gone.

FATHER: It's not the end of the world.

SON: It is. For me it is. I cannot afford life without their pension. Couldn't they move to the fuckin' retirement village? To save us embarrassment. I'll be eight soon. Shame. Shame on you and you, Grandmother! And to think that I loved you.

GRANDFATHER: I've had it. I'm not waiting.

GRANDMOTHER'S VOICE: Wait a second. I've had it, too. Wait for me. I'll be there in no time at all. Can't they leave us in peace? So we can wait to see the end? [*To* SON] And to think that I loved you? I'm coming!

GRANDMOTHER *enters. Followed by* DAUGHTER.

GRANDMOTHER *chains herself to the lamppost and frees the urn.*

DAUGHTER: I can't sleep.

EVERYMAN *enters as* PSYCHIATRIST.

EVERYMAN/PSYCHIATRIST: Insomnia. People who can't sleep suffer from unpleasant thoughts, intrusive thoughts, excessive worry, uncontrollable anxiety, extreme tension… It all results in emotional distress…

FATHER: Sounds like me. I suffer from all the above symptoms, yet I sleep like a log.

EVERYMAN/PSYCHIATRIST: You're not an insomniac, then. You're just your typical nervous wreck. I cannot help you.

DAUGHTER: Can you help me?

EVERYMAN/PSYCHIATRIST: No, I cannot, but if you follow me, I know someone who was a woman who is a gay man who can help you.

DAUGHTER: Mother?

EVERYMAN/PSYCHIATRIST: Yes. Mother. He helped me.

MOTHER *crosses.*

MOTHER: Follow me, both of you. I can help each of you.

They follow her.

GRANDMOTHER: She will kill them both. They won't see the end.

FATHER: 'He' will kill them both. Not 'she'. You heard.

SON: I am going with them. I want her… I want him to help me, too. I need a father figure. A proper father figure.

SON *moves to follow them.*

FATHER: You're going nowhere! There is only one father figure for you and if I can't have you, then nobody else will. I will kill you.

SON: You will regret it.

GRANDMOTHER: You will regret it.

GRANDFATHER: You will regret it.

FATHER: I will regret it, but what the hell.

FATHER *kills* SON.

He immediately regrets it.

I regret it, however I need some privacy for my solo piece.

DEAD SON: I told you! Poor Father…

GRANDMOTHER: Oh, shut up and be gone!

DEAD SON: I'll be gone, when ready, alright?

GRANDMOTHER: Alright. I still have a soft spot for you.

FATHER: Do you understand me?

GRANDFATHER *and* GRANDMOTHER *understand. They nod their heads.*

GRANDFATHER: Deliver in peace! We understand. Your dead son will be gone, soon.

FATHER*'s solo piece: 'Remember the Flower Children Coming?'...*

FATHER: Look at him. He looks so peaceful now. [*Pause.*] It was twenty-two, maybe forty-four years ago. We were in a foreign city. It was cold and sunny. A group of young women checked into the same hotel. They all looked gorgeous. We were seated in a hotel restaurant... Was it a hotel? Maybe some kind of a dormitory. Some group accommodation place, like a student house, a youth hostel... Yes, and we were seated in a canteen behind a glass wall... the glass wall was separating us from all those young beauties. They were definitely a sports team: a volleyball team, not a hockey team, no... they were too slim for hockey. And tall, they were. They were not wearing any uniformed outfits, though. Most of them were wearing skirts, long dresses, floral dresses. They were joking and laughing and... [*Pause.*] I forgot... One of them noticed me staring at them and she told her two friends. She pointed at me and they all smiled, they stood in a row and raised their skirts a little bit, in a cabaret-like mocking gesture, to show me their long legs. I blushed and turned back to the table to face my family again. The girls laughed. My family didn't laugh...

DEAD SON: I cannot listen to this, Father. I'm gone.

GRANDFATHER: You better be. It is his solo piece.

DEAD SON *is gone. It seems that he is gone for good.*

FATHER: Was it the Olympics? Some sporting games? So many young, beautiful people in that foreign city. And police. Everywhere. Everyone smiling. All day long I couldn't think of anything else, but those playful girls at the dormitory. I didn't go with my family for the sightseeing tour of the foreign city. I stayed in. I said I had a headache. I used to have severe headaches in those days, though I am not sure now, if I truly had a headache that day. I remember seeing my wife, my woman, boarding the Foreign City Tour Bus among other passengers. She was a beautiful woman. Exceptionally beautiful. The image of her among other passengers crowding, pushing each other gently, almost rubbing their bodies against each other as they negotiated the steps to the bus, that picture aroused me. At that very moment I wanted her to stay with me… and to make love… but the door closed and the bus took off. My woman was looking at me from the window as the Foreign City Tour Bus drove away. [*Pause.*] I turned back and found myself face to face with the smiling girl. Long dark hair, brown and green eyes, perfectly shaped little nose pointing upwards, beautiful hands. 'You don't want to see the city with your family?' she asked. 'I don't feel well. I have a headache,' I answered. She looked me straight in the eye and then reached out and touched my temple. The other girls were looking at us. 'This should help you,' she said. 'Have you ever tried this?' She held out a pill. An ordinary-looking pill. 'Thank you,' I said. And I swallowed the pill as if it was Holy Communion. [*Pause.*] I was in a large hall full of beds and large pillows. There were two girls making love on one of the beds. There were two girls next to me. There were more people around, but I cannot remember them. I was looking around for my woman. I wanted to see her making love. But she wasn't there… I needed her in order to tell what was good and what was bad… If she was there, and I wanted her there badly, if she was there I knew I would be alright there. It would all be good… But she wasn't there and I felt guilty… Everyone around was making love and I felt guilty… because I couldn't see my woman making love to anyone… I cried like a baby… I didn't know… [*Pause.*] The City Tour Bus never came back—or did it? It was bombed that day, or was it? All those terrorists, all those attacks… One cannot remember them all. [*Pause.*] The flower children were always against war. They saved so many lives. They saved my life, but they didn't save the bus that got bombed. They couldn't save all the buses, I guess.

MOTHER *enters.*

MOTHER: I cannot save them all.

FATHER: Do you remember the flower children?

MOTHER: What are you talking about? What children?

FATHER: Never mind.

MOTHER: I just killed the gay man I loved and in the process I also got rid of that young woman who called me Mother.

FATHER: You got rid of her? You mean: she is dead?

MOTHER: I guess so.

FATHER: So, how many of us left? I am getting confused.

MOTHER: Does it matter? Who wants to face the apocalypse, anyway?

GRANDFATHER & GRANDMOTHER: I do.

GRANDMOTHER: That's the point of the whole exercise. To miss it now would be stupid. After what we've been through.

GRANDFATHER: And all the money we've spent, so far.

FATHER: I killed that young man, who called me Father.

MOTHER: You're my man, then! [*Pause.*] I remember you! You want to dance?

FATHER: Do you mind if I swing a little?

MOTHER: Swing all you want, baby. It may be our final swing before we hang.

FATHER: You may be right about that. I didn't want you to have them if I couldn't have them… Nobody will… there is only one father.

MOTHER: Only one!

They dance.

GRANDMOTHER *and* GRANDFATHER *join in the dance.*

EVERYMAN *enters as himself.*

EVERYMAN: Parties of up to five people keep gathering as the final countdown begins… No-one wants to miss the once-in-a-lifetime opportunity to witness the end of the world. All the TV and radio stations are bracing themselves for the big… what?… bang?… blackout?… fire?… tornado?… big what? The live coverage has already started. The ratings will surely skyrocket. It is said that it may outrate 'Big Brother' by approximately four hundred and fifty percent. Can you imagine that? Un-bloody-believable! TV and radio equipment has been set up to run without human supervision, so that the coverage will continue even after we are gone. There is a point to it. Of course. Some of us have prepared for doomsday by building family bunkers. Pole to Pole Shelter Constructors have reported that demand has tripled. End of the World souvenirs are selling hot. The Final Judgment business is thriving, getting better minute-by-minute. Are we ready? Below the meadows of Nebraska, as I speak, the mini underground bunker city fills with the lives of the chosen ones. A fitting retirement village, indeed. Are we ready for today? For as one famous woman sang in her coarse voice: 'There is no fuckin' tomorrow. There is only today. For tomorrow never comes to Man.' [*Pause.*] Today: the same day that Brutus killed Caesar, the same day that the united forces of nations overthrew the hated Colonel, the 'Bear of an Acid King' died ending for good the flower children's era of revolution, the same day that a starstruck astronomer departed on his last journey of discovery, a journey of no return, through the rings of Uranus, the same day that red poppies drank the blood of dead soldiers fighting the enemy in a foreign country, the same day that the *Titanic* finally sunk… the same day… or is it the same night? Today the world ends. [*Pause.*] Yes, everyday, somewhere a Brutus kills a Caesar, and every day a world comes to an end. Our world will stop today. So, don't misbehave. Follow these three simple rules: NO FARTING! NO BURPING! NO SPITTING! So that we can say our 'goodbyes' in style and with dignity. Let's dance. Let's dance. Let's dance.

MOTHER, FATHER, GRANDMOTHER *and* GRANDFATHER *are still dancing.*

They stop dancing.

Third Quarter ends here.

FINAL QUARTER

MOTHER, FATHER, GRANDMOTHER *and* GRANDFATHER *are dancing again.*

MOTHER *stops dancing.*

MOTHER: That's it.

GRANDFATHER *howls like a wounded wolf.*

FATHER *stops dancing.*

FATHER: That's it.

GRANDFATHER *and* GRANDMOTHER *stop dancing.*

GRANDMOTHER: Go and hang yourselves.

MOTHER *and* FATHER *consider.*

MOTHER: Can I ask for something before we go and hang ourselves?

GRANDMOTHER: It depends.

MOTHER: No it doesn't depend on anything. It is my final wish and final wishes are always granted.

GRANDMOTHER: You asked, I answered.

MOTHER: I didn't ask. It was a figure of speech. You were to say, 'Yes'. 'Yes' was all I asked you for.

GRANDMOTHER: See: you asked.

MOTHER *roars like a lion.*

FATHER: She asked you for just one word: 'Yes'. So, say it!

GRANDMOTHER: Yes.

MOTHER: Thank you. There is one thing I have to settle before I will be gone. Before we will be gone.

EVERYMAN *enters as* POLICEMAN.

EVERYMAN/POLICEMAN: You have three minutes. Three minutes each.

MOTHER: It will be my solo piece. I don't wish to share it with anyone.

EVERYMAN/POLICEMAN: Sure thing. You understand? Any objections?

FATHER: No. I understand.

EVERYMAN/POLICEMAN: Proceed.

MOTHER: Thank you.

Pause.

MOTHER*'s solo piece 'Remember the Fuckin' Meditation?'...*

It was eleven years ago. Twenty-two years ago? Hard to say now. Could be more, could be less. Feels like yesterday. When he finished, he collapsed on me like a heavy log. Like a very heavy log. I had needed a distraction. Do you know what a distraction is?

EVERYMAN: [*as himself*] It is an unnoticed transfer of attention from one object to another.

MOTHER: It is an unnoticed transfer of attention from one object to another. Exactly. [*Pause.*] It's dark, so I cannot see him. I can only feel him. I can smell him. I need a distraction, so I'm not thinking of this heavy former world champion shot-putter sweating it out on me. In and out. Up and down. In and out. Inhale and exhale. Inhale and exhale. Heavy breathing becomes deep breathing. It becomes a rhythm. I concentrate on the rhythm. The rhythm. The rhythm takes me away. I forget where I am and what's going on. I start daydreaming: I am on a boat on a peaceful lake. The sun. The sun's rays blazing down. It's hot. The sun lifts me up and I travel in its outstretched arms. It's bliss. I forget that I have a body. What body? I forget who I am. I am one with the sun. I want to stay forever. To be no-one. Or not to be. Not at all. [*Pause.*] I didn't want to come back. I was meditating. Like in a yoga class: lay back and close your eyes. Yes. He was fucking me and I was meditating. Meditation was my everyday escape. My mind wandered off every time he climbed on me. Fuckin' meditation saved my life. He was a good man. He loved me. How was I to tell him that I wasn't there? That I never loved him? [*Pause.*] That day, when I returned to my body, he was heavy. Heavier than usual. I didn't move at first and I realised that his sweat was cold. He was cold. He was lying on me and he wasn't breathing. It took me a while to realise that he was dead. As I lay there it occurred to me that I too wanted to feel what it is to be a man sweating it out on a delicate body. I wanted to fuck and to come and to collapse, exhausted, on the tiny absent-minded body lying beneath. And I wanted that tiny body to be that of a man. I wanted my revenge on my big dead shot-putter world champion. I wanted my revenge on all men. I wanted to be a man. And I never wanted to marry again.

MOTHER *finishes her solo piece.*

Why did you marry, you two?

GRANDFATHER: [*hissing like a snake*] Ask her.

GRANDMOTHER: Convenience, I guess. My partner died and his partner died. We were single. We had the same grandchildren. We had you. I mean, he had him and I had you. We were already a family… we shared you, we shared grandchildren… It seemed less confusing to just get married and to carry on like before.

MOTHER: Before? Carry on like before? What do you mean?

GRANDMOTHER: Nothing. Shut up. And go and hang yourself as you promised.

MOTHER *goes to hang herself.*

You, too. Weren't you to hang together, lovebirds?

FATHER: Oh, yes. Of course. Sorry. She probably forgot…

GRANDFATHER *roars like a lion.*

FATHER *runs after* MOTHER *to hang himself with her.*

GRANDFATHER: What do you mean: 'like before'?

GRANDMOTHER: Oh, I don't know. Nothing, really. [*Pause.*] For things to remain the same. Between us.

GRANDFATHER: Exactly: 'between us'? There was nothing between us before.

GRANDMOTHER: Yes. And we have managed to keep it that way, haven't we?

GRANDFATHER: [*roaring like a lion*] True. We have. Things may change slightly… Now that there are only the two of us left.

EVERYMAN: [*as* EVERYMAN] Three.

SON *enters carrying a soapbox.*

Three of you…

DAUGHTER *enters.*

Four of you.

DAUGHTER: With you included, we will make the proper crowd of five for the end.

EVERYMAN: With me included, it will definitely be a 'five-plus…' crowd. Illegal. I am Everyman. I am everyone else. I will keep my distance.

SON *jumps on the box.*

DAUGHTER: Where did you get this box from?

SON: Found it underneath our hanging mother.

DAUGHTER: Now I recognise it. This is our father's box. There were two. Where is the other one?

SON: Underneath our hanging father.

DAUGHTER: That'd be right. I will go and get it.

SON: What do you need it for?

DAUGHTER: My solo piece, like you.

SON: Oh, I see. Freedom of Speech Act. But be careful, they might fall… the line might snap… the branches might break… anything. Today is Black Friday!

EVERYMAN: Tuesday.

SON: Black Tuesday. Never heard of it.

EVERYMAN: The world ends on Tuesday. [*Pause.*] Never mind.

DAUGHTER *exits.*

SON*'s solo piece: 'Remember the Day We Believed in God?'...*

GRANDFATHER: What god?

GRANDMOTHER: Does it matter? His god.

SON: Shut up. It is my solo piece. [*Pause.*] It doesn't matter as there is only one God or there are many gods, if you need them. I believed in God. It was seven or seventeen years ago. Yes. It is quite possible that this story happened before I was born. Maybe I was waiting to be born. Who knows? The spring was in full swing. It could have been summer by the way things looked, but the calendar is never wrong. The calendar indicated spring. The awakening. Trees blossoming, birds chirping, dogs pairing, humans matching… All the little ones were wearing white outfits and lining up at the heavy wooden gates of the temple. The gates were open and all the little ones could see a beam of sunlight shooting across the temple's vast space to land on a magnificently carved altar at the far end. The little ones knew that soon they would be allowed to step inside and they would be invited to unite with the Almighty through the holy ritual of initiation. They longed for it and they feared it. Such was the tradition and the rule: 'You shall fear me but you shall long for me' spelled the inscription across the base of the altar. Behind the altar stood the priest. The little ones could not see him in the shadows, though they could see the sun reflecting off his golden rings and bracelets. They were to kiss one of the rings during the ceremony. On the other side of the open gate stood all the big ones. The adults. Each had a gift for their own little one. The sight of all the big ones was reassuring. All the big ones were there. All, but mine. There was no-one there for me. I waited and waited. I was letting the other little ones take my place in the queue, hoping that someone would show up for me. No-one did. I was the only one not to get the gift. That day I made myself a promise, that I shall never ever fear God again. The inscription was for those who didn't believe. I understood that no matter what happened to me, if I believed in God I shall fear no death, for there was no death as such, the way I saw it. If my soul was immortal, then my body could make peace with the dying and the pain. My own self would travel on with my soul.

I smiled to my thoughts. At that very moment I heard a slap echoing through the temple and I felt a stinging sensation in my left ear. The priest had smacked me… for smiling. He'd realised I didn't fear God. I guess God had wanted me to cry, and I cried after that smack, but I never feared God. I feared the priest. I believed in God. I felt strong. [*Pause.*] I never felt the same strength again. [*Pause.*] If my soul were mortal then it'd die the moment my body died. [*Pause.*] I've always wanted to be there when the end comes. Because I've always wanted to meet my God. I've always wondered whether or not my God has a beard. On one hand all gods seem to have beards, but I think they got it wrong. I think that my God is clean-shaven. [*Pause.*] I don't believe in the end coming to us from the outside. It will come from within. [*Pause.*] I can die over and over again. They can kill me as many times as they want to, but they won't take my life. Only I can take my own life.

SON *finishes his solo piece.*

DAUGHTER *comes back with a soapbox and a sign: 'THAT'S IT. THIS IS THE END!'*

Do you remember the day we believed in God?

DAUGHTER *raises the sign.*

GRANDFATHER *growls like a dog.*

GRANDMOTHER: You must be kidding. That's it? This is the end.

GRANDFATHER *and* GRANDMOTHER *laugh.*

GRANDMOTHER & GRANDFATHER: Ha, ha, ha!

DAUGHTER *raises the sign again.*

GRANDFATHER, GRANDMOTHER *and* SON *laugh louder.*

GRANDMOTHER, GRANDFATHER & SON: Ha! Ha! Ha!
SON: Are you serious? Don't you have anything more original to say?
DAUGHTER: My solo piece.

GRANDMOTHER, GRANDFATHER *and* SON *laugh hysterically.*

GRANDMOTHER, GRANDFATHER & SON: Hahahahaha!

EVERYMAN *enters as* POLICEMAN. *He blows his whistle.*

The laughter stops.

EVERYMAN/POLICEMAN: Dance everyone!

Everyone dances.

EVERYMAN *takes his* POLICEMAN *hat off.*

EVERYMAN: [*as* EVERYMAN] Remember what the wise man says: the end of the world will be announced to a packed auditorium in a theatre, where a show will be cancelled due to the end of the world. And the audience will explode with laughter. And they will applaud the announcer, as they will take his announcement for a prime joke. Kind of a prologue in front of a drawn curtain. The end before the story really begins. Now, that's funny!

EVERYMAN *puts on his* POLICEMAN *hat. He blows his whistle. They stop dancing.*

EVERYMAN/POLICEMAN: Proceed. Your solo piece!
DAUGHTER: Yes. My solo piece.

She jumps on the soapbox.

DAUGHTER*'s solo piece: 'Remember me dance?'...*

I always thought that my solo piece would be a dance number, so I am not really prepared to talk. But, I guess it would be impossible to dance on a soapbox. [*Pause.*] The dance I would like to dance tells a story. So, I will have to tell you my dance, this story, which happened maybe yesterday, maybe a hundred years ago. It may be happening now, as I speak, even though it's set in the past. Everything is set in the past now: there was a man whose actions brought death upon many people. Many of them his brothers and sisters. He wasn't concerned with their deaths, because he was only acting under the strict orders of his superiors, who acted upon the strict rules of their faith, which in turn was based upon the strict laws of nature bestowed upon them by their gods and revealed in their *Book of EVERYTHING*. So the man prayed in the morning, killed during the day, ate in the evening and slept at night… he woke up and he ate and killed again. The man didn't think. But one day the wheel of fortune turned and his superiors deserted him and he was left on his own with his actions. [*Pause.*] I will demonstrate the turning wheel of fortune movement, now. It is my favourite bit: the 'Wheel of Fortune'.

DAUGHTER *gets off the soapbox and does the announcement.*

The 'Wheel of Fortune' into the 'Deserted Murderer'.

DAUGHTER *performs a little dramatic dance starting with a cartwheel flip. She finishes in the deserted murderer posture. She bows. She gets back on the box.*

It's called the cartwheel. In India it is called *Talavilasitam karana.* Capoeira has a similar move—they call it the *aú.* It's my favourite bit. Even without music. [*Pause.*] At my dance school, there was a dance master, who made us practise martial arts to music. After months of practice one of the students asked him, 'Master, what is the difference between practising with music and practising without music?' Master looked at him and said, 'Begin'. The student started the routine. Then the Master stopped the music. They practised in silence. After a minute or so, the Master started the music again. 'Keep going,' he said. They practised to the music. 'Now you know the difference,' he said.

Pause.

GRANDFATHER: And what happened to the man who was deserted by his gods?

DAUGHTER: Without his superiors and their gods the deserted murderer started to fear. He was made to face the consequences of his actions. He was tried and sentenced to death.

GRANDFATHER *howls with fear.*

GRANDMOTHER *slaps him on the head.*

DAUGHTER *raises the sign again: 'THAT'S IT. THIS IS THE END!'*

That's all I know. That's my whole dance. Thank you for letting me share it with you. I know no more.

GRANDMOTHER: I want to know what's next. I don't buy into the vague and rushed ending. What are you going to do about it, young lady? You are not going to drop dead on me, are you?

DAUGHTER: But of course, I am.

DAUGHTER *cuts her wrists and drops dead.*

SON: She told you: 'That's it!' And she is damn right. You are bad, bad people, you know. You don't want to follow the path of many and all. You put shame on us, on our family. You deprive us of your own benefits. You won't force us to be gone, but we are ready. Like Mother and Father, like Daughter and Son: we will be gone. She is damn right. I am going to drop dead on you, too.

SON *cuts his wrists and drops dead.*

GRANDMOTHER: I want to know what happens to the deserted man!

EVERYMAN: [*as* EVERYMAN] Nobody knows for sure, but the most likely scenario is that he asked for clemency. Wouldn't it be wonderful to moderate the severity of his punishment, to show forbearance, compassion, or even forgiveness in judging such a deserted murderer? But: no. The same gods who protected him, when he was dutifully fulfilling his service to his superiors, the same gods declined to pardon him. They were only gods, after all. They had too much to lose. And what is the loss of one life against that of thousands. The *Book of EVERYTHING* is very explicit in its laws: 'Rule number one: Don't kill.' And 'Rule number two: Kill if necessary.' 'Rule number three: Apply rules one and two with a thorough understanding of the overall situation.' So, he was to hang. The usual time for hanging is said to be 6:00 p.m.

GRANDMOTHER: What's the time now?

EVERYMAN: Quarter to.

GRANDFATHER *howls with fear.*

Any last wishes? A shot of vodka? A special meal? A letter to the family? Perhaps your favourite porn film? Or just a confession? These and other questions would be routinely asked by the executioner before… you know.

GRANDFATHER: Shut up, please! It's very unsettling. Your commentary is very disturbing.

GRANDMOTHER: Do you think we can still make it to the retirement compound, before it's too late?

EVERYMAN: Let me see.

EVERYMAN *becomes* SOCIAL WORKER.

EVERYMAN/SOCIAL WORKER: It is still possible… theoretically. However there is a catch. I have two letters here. One of them is ordering you to move to your retirement village immediately. This is in case you refuse to go there and still carry on with your silly childish rebellion. And we have the means, of course, to force you to move in. The second letter deprives you forever of any and all rights regarding access to retirement accommodation. This is to be referred to in the event that you change your mind and decide that you belong with your likes after all, and decide to move into the retirement village of your own volition. You see, no matter what you choose, we are prepared to react accordingly.

GRANDMOTHER: Sounds great! You know, with so much fuss about the end coming and the judgment day being upon us… and blah-blah-blah… too much ado about nothing… I think we'd be much better off if we stop protesting and move in straight away. Not much time left.

EVERYMAN/SOCIAL WORKER: I understand. You want to move in. In that case you get the second letter: 'You are being stripped of all rights for retirement accommodation…'

GRANDMOTHER: No, no, no. You misunderstood—I mean: I misunderstood you. It's all okay. Officially, we are still protesting, so you can feel free to force us to move in now. You know what I mean. We don't want to move in, so we can move in, because you have to force us to do so and everyone is happy.

EVERYMAN/SOCIAL WORKER: So, you understand, why I cannot force you to move in—because you want me to force you to move in. Plan B stands. You can forget the accommodation. No further discussion will be entered into. Sign here. And here.

GRANDMOTHER *signs.*

And you. Here and here.

GRANDFATHER *signs.*

EVERYMAN *becomes himself.*

EVERYMAN: The sentence stands as delivered upon the first hearing. The appeal is rejected.

EVERYMAN *exits.*

MOTHER *and* FATHER *enter with nooses around their necks, looking rather pale and dead-ish.*

MOTHER: You silly old buggers!

FATHER: You allowed yourselves to be manipulated like little kids. Though you deserved it all.

DAUGHTER *and* SON *come back to life.*

SON: I was hoping you'd be firmer. There was still a chance.

GRANDFATHER *hisses like a snake.*

It's all your fault.

GRANDMOTHER: It is. You can't deny that. [*Pause.*] I thought you were all dead.

MOTHER, FATHER, DAUGHTER & SON: We are, silly!

GRANDFATHER *growls defensively.*

GRANDMOTHER: Never mind.

GRANDFATHER: I give you my permission, now.

GRANDMOTHER: To do what?

GRANDFATHER: Whatever you want. You kept asking, remember?

GRANDMOTHER: No. But that's nice of you, anyway. At least we are here together. Together till the very end. Like a family.

SON: We are family.

FATHER: After all.

DAUGHTER: Do you know if the end comes with music or without music?

FATHER: What's the difference?

They all look at him.

DAUGHTER: You'll see. [*Pause.*] And if there is music to come—I wonder what kind of music?

They all turn away and stare upstage.

MOTHER: What time is it?

EVERYMAN: It's nearing the end of the final quarter. [*Pause.*] The ending music is up to you. Choose your favourite. I will provide the lyrics.

The chosen music starts to play.

Final Quarter ends here.

EPILOGUE/SWIMDOWN

EVERYMAN: Remember: no farting, no burping and no spitting! Otherwise: you can dance, you can sing, you can do as you please, because:

The Ten Commandments monument in the old courthouse in Alabama: there will be no more!
Devil saying, 'Goodnight, darling' in Tasmania: there will be no more!

MOTHER, FATHER, DAUGHTER, SON, GRANDMOTHER *and* GRANDFATHER *dance.*

Let me explain: you were never given Freedom. You were given a chance at Freedom. You weren't given Wisdom. You were given the option to gain Wisdom. This world may be trustworthy yet it is capricious. It may be merciful while it is still unforgiving. Not bad, not greedy. Not spiteful, not jealous! Simply: unforgiving! And the only one you have.
Those who were hurt shall fight back. By all means and with all their might.
Those who were wronged shall be rewarded. The last ones will come first.
Those who are hungry… well, there is still some time for a quick visit to the nearest takeaway shop. Fast food is your only option now. It is getting really late…

EVERYMAN *goes to the ashtray stand.*

He picks up the cigar he left there in the beginning.

EVERYMAN *draws the curtains.*

EVERYMAN *stands in front of the curtains smoking the cigar.*

Ladies and gentlemen. That's it! There will be no more. This is the end. [*Pause.*] And: Cut!

EVERYMAN *puts the cigar out. Lights out.*

THE END

presents

Everyman & The Pole Dancers

1–5 and 7–11 October 2014

Performers:
Everyman: **Maude Davey**
The Grandmother: **Jane Bayly**
The Grandfather: **Matt Crosby**
The Mother: **Kathleen Doyle**
The Father: **Kazuto Shimamoto**
The Daughter: **Keina Denda**
The Son: **Reece Vella**

Writer/Director: **Lech Mackiewicz**
Co-producer: **Matt Crosby**
Visual installation artist: **Naomi Ota**
Composer: **Noriko Tadano**
Lighting designer: **Shane Grant**
Production manager: **Lara Week**
Stage manager: **Carly McGregor**

WRITER/DIRECTOR'S NOTE

I struggle to remember what happened three years ago. A year ago. A month. I struggle to remember what exactly happened yesterday. If our lives are indeed like rivers then our memories will be always shifting and we will have to make a constant effort to remember what exactly has happened to us. What currents brought us to our present situation. And depending on the context, the memories will change in an effort to justify our past actions. What we considered good yesterday becomes politically and morally incorrect today.

This world's death is an ongoing process. Worlds end everyday. My worlds consist of people—my worlds come and go. They overlap, they unite and part. My family is my world. My culture is my world. My words, too. The importance of each of the worlds differ. As does the impact they have on us. We bear the consequences. Some of my worlds have ended and some new ones have arisen a few times since I wrote this play.

One can say that I've been lucky because I have been given a few lives. Yes, quite a few lives. Lucky indeed. Though nobody ever asked me whether I was willing to participate in that relay of new chances. Hypothetically, it is quite possible that given a choice, I would be happy to settle with many less options. Maybe just one world would suffice? I will never know.

Why exactly did I write *Everyman & The Pole Dancers*? I struggle to remember. It was in a different world. My own note says that I wrote it in reaction to the tragedy of the Japanese tsunami. That tragedy directly ignited the writing—this is true. I think. I remember seeing masses of dark water swallowing houses, trees, roads, carrying cars and human bodies. Thousands of worlds ended that day. The only way to save them is to remember. But can we trust our memories? Historians and politicians, public and social media manipulate the past and the memories. It is sad or funny, depending on the way we look at it. Maybe both. We often laugh at our collective social dementia. This is often a choice we make in the face of an awkward situation. Awkward truth. A denial of sorts. A tragedy with a clown's face. It is funny.

So why not laugh at yet another end of the world! The story is simple, if a little bit absurd: Three generations of one family are trying to settle their earthly matters before the imminent end. Everyman guides them (and us) through the final stages of their existence and helps them to say their goodbyes with dignity—to say their goodbyes before the curtains are drawn on the old world they knew. Grandfather and Grandmother rebel against their coming retirement accommodation causing their grandchildren and children to pull every trick in the book to get their Grandparents' pension. In the process they perform their 'solo pieces', remembering the best and the worst days of their lives... and they dance, as only dancing can save them from the deadly stress of facing the end of the world, which they are so keen to witness.

This is a comedy. Apocalyptic, but still a comedy.

Directing it now I shall be trying to re-visit my own past, our own past and to see the world we are waving goodbye to in a different light. Figuratively speaking. I hope that all of us, the company and the spectators alike, will be able to recognise that world.

Lech Mackiewicz and Reece Vella. (Photo: Adam Hanuszkiewicz)

LECH MACKIEWICZ

WRITER / DIRECTOR

Lech Mackiewicz has written and directed his European nuanced theatre in Poland, Japan and Australia with a particular interest in notions of the fall, the perversions of the family and the memory play. His main influences are Fellini and Tadeusz Kantor; ritual, memory and pathos are central to his vision. His work relies on non-literal design. In Japan Lech directed with the Suzuki Company Of Toga (SCOT) and Actor's Company Mito. International festivals include Japan, Melbourne, Krakow. Lech co-founded Auto Da Fe in 1987. He has been supported by the Australia Council, Playking Foundation, received several awards for his film and theatre in Poland and Australia and graduated from the National State Academy of Theatre in Cracow (Poland) in 1983. Credits include: *King Lear*, Playbox (Melbourne Festival) Japan and Korea; *The Hour Before My Brother Dies* for Jaracza Theatre (Poland), *Krapps's Last Tape*, Auto Da Fe (Poland, Australia, Japan); *Felliniada* (Belvoir); *So Called K*, Mito Acting Company (Japan); *Beckett in Circles*, SCOT (Japan); *An Oak Tree*, Teatr Wegierki (Poland); *NaGL*, for Teatr Auto Da Fe (Sydney); *Ditto, A Story*, La Mama (Melbourne); *Kafka Tanczy,* Teatr Zydowski (Warsaw).

http://lechmackiewicz.com

NAOMI OTA

VISUAL INSTALLATION ARTIST

Naomi Ota is an installation artist whose work uses fibrous materials. Naomi often draws on images and memories from the natural world and from the earth; places connected to emotional memory, places faraway in the imagination and calling on her memories of growing-up in Japan. Naomi's works have been exhibited in various exhibitions in Australia, Singapore, Belgium, France, UK and Japan. Her works are in public collections, which include National Gallery of Victoria, Museum of Victoria, Art Bank and Kyoto Nishijin Textile Industrial Association. Naomi has extended her practice to include work on a range of national and international projects spanning butoh, contemporary dance, intercultural theatre, and experiential arts projects where she contributes interactive design and spatial elements. Her process is intuitive and collaborative. The result is often to lead the viewer to a more interactive sense of the performance space and an understanding of how expressive qualities of performance are multidimensional. Naomi has PhD in textile art from RMIT University and MAs in fine arts from RMIT University and the Kyoto City University of Arts, Japan. www.naomiota.com

NORIKO TADANO
COMPOSER

Noriko Tadano plays both traditional Japanese folk songs (Minyo) as well as original pieces on the Tsugaru Shamisen (Japanese Banjo). She has been playing shamisen since she was 6 years old and has performed in Japan, Europe, Canada, Tonga, Fiji and at festivals and events all over Australia. While traditional Minyo depicts the life and feelings of 'older' Japan, centring around the themes of love, family and the close connection with nature, Noriko's original pieces explore feelings and experiences through melodic notes and heart pounding beats.

https://myspace.com/norikotadano

SHANE GRANT
LIGHTING DESIGNER

Shane Grant graduated from the Victorian College of the Arts in 1994, specialising in lighting design for theatre dance and music. Since then he has designed for some of Victoria's most innovative companies including: Keene Taylor theatre project, Not Yet it's Difficult, Melbourne Chorale, Ranters Theatre, Playbox Theatre and Yumi Umiumare. Shane was nominated for a Green Room award in 2011 for his lighting design for Inotrope's version of *The Tempest* at Theatreworks. Shane was the technical manager for Gasworks theatre between 1996 and 2000. He toured internationally with Strange Fruit 1999–2005 as Lighting Designer/production manager/safety officer. Shane is currently a company director of Metanoia Theatre and the technical manager of the Mechanics Institute Theatre in Brunswick.

LARA WEEK
PRODUCTION MANAGER

Lara Week is a producer and designer for performance. Her background includes: co-creating monthly community music event Deja in her home city of Sydney; leading play-building workshops for children with Galli Theatre, Berlin; making costumes for a children's program in the Israeli Opera; and working with children in a youth club for refugees in Tel Aviv. Since 2011, Lara has been associate producer for Tribal Soul, producing community programs and original performances in Zimbabwe, Mozambique, the Netherlands, UK, and Australia. In 2013, Lara completed her PG Dip in Performance Creation (Design) at the Victorian College of the Arts. She is dedicated to creating spaces where people with different skills and perspectives can share ideas and produce work together.
www.laraweek.com

CARLY MCGREGOR
STAGE MANAGER

Carly McGregor is a freelance Stage Manager and Lighting and Sound Operator. She came of age in England, but quickly realised the error of her parents' ways and migrated to our sunny land. Her background is in the technical and management fields and since running away to join the circus has realised that her future is in the arts. Her most recent credit was as Stage Manager and Lighting Operator for *Missfits* at LaMama.

MAUDE DAVEY

EVERYMAN

Maude Davey trained at VCA and has worked as an actor, director and writer for over twenty-five years, her primary focus being new work. Her most recent work was a solo retrospective, called *My Life in the Nude* at La Mama Theatre, which toured in 2014. Recent directing work includes *Evolution, Revolution and the Mail Order Bride* by Zulya Kamalova (fortyfivedownstairs); *Just an Old Fashioned Grrrl!* by Danielle Asciak and *Herstory* for Imogen Kelly. Much of her work has a community focus. Although based in Melbourne, she has an ongoing relationship with Vitalstatistix Theatre Company in Adelaide, with whom she has produced such events as *Second to None*, an Indigenous and Maritime history of Port Adelaide, and the *Cutaway* series (2011–2013). She has collaborated often with Finucane & Smith as a member of The Burlesque Hour ensemble, touring nationally and internationally for the last ten years.

JANE BAYLY

THE GRANDMOTHER

Jane Bayly is as an actor/singer, theatre maker and teacher. A founding member of a cappella theatre company Crying in Public Places, she co-devised several shows and toured extensively. With Carole Patullo she made *Button*, a play with songs selected for the 2013 VCE Playlist (La Mama Courthouse). Recent performances include *Dust* (Hubcap Productions, national tour), *Care Instructions* (with Aphids/Malthouse, Transit VI Festival, Denmark), *Miss Hewett's Shenanigans* and *The Chapel Perilous* (Perilous Productions). Other theatre includes *homeland* and *neither lost nor found* with the Keene/Taylor Theatre Project, *Blabbermouth* (Arena Theatre/MTC), *King Lear* and *The Newspaper of Claremont St* for Playbox/Malthouse, *The Women There*, *Brecht x2* (Arena Theatre), *Infectiou$* (Crying Out Loud), *Viva La Vida: Frida Kahlo* (Handspan), *STOMP!* (Yes/No People) and *The Sapphires* creative development (MTC). Recent screen work includes *The Time of Our Lives*, *The Broken Shore*, *Offspring*, *The Slap*, *The Wedding Party* and *The Hollow Men*. Jane teaches for theatre companies, schools, community and corporate organisations, and was Director of the Monash Schools' Theatre Festival from 2008-2012.

MATT CROSBY

THE GRANDFATHER / CO-PRODUCER

Matt Crosby has collaborated with Asian artists since the Playbox/ SCOT *Chronicles of Macbeth* in 1992. Afterwards, he received Japan Foundation Fellowship and Asialink residencies, ArtsVic and Ozco grants as well as philanthropic support to further his interest in the history, theory and especially practice of Asian performance and in particular Japanese theatre. A turning point for him was the collaboration, over three months, with Singapore's Ong Keng Sen in *Sandakan Threnody* (Singapore, Brisbane, Melbourne festivals), which led to the broadening of his cross-media pursuit and the terrain on which he collaborated. Joining Lech and Auto Da Fe is another touchstone. And how could he forget working with Suzanne Chaundy on *The Maids* at La Mama? Matt is a graduate of NIDA 1981, has studied Japanese at RMIT and holds a DipEd. https://sites.google.com/site/crosbeee/

KATHLEEN DOYLE

THE MOTHER

Kathleen Doyle's training includes over 14 years with the Suzuki Actor Training Method, and over 3 years intensive dance training in Japan with Butoh/Contemporary dancers, Ohno Kazuo, Kasai Akira, FukuharaTetsuro, and Uesugi Mitsuyo. Her most recent works include *The Space Between Performance Collective's Thing with Feathers* (2013), *Ten Worlds* (2013) and *Creature* (2011). She was an actor with Suzuki Tadashi's company, training and rehearsing with the company (2004-2005) and performing in Suzuki's *King Lear* and *Antigone*. She was an actor with Ku Na'uka (2002-2003), and performed the role of Aegisthus in *Elektra*, Dionysus in *The Bacchae* and Chorus in *Mahabharata*. She was a collaborator with company Image Opera in Traktor – Heiner Müller Festival and danced under choreographer Ioanna Garagoni in Rose Dies, and choreographer Sanari Tetsuo in *Fantasy Virus*. She was Assistant Director of Dance for Tokyo Space Dance (2001–2003).

KAZUTO SHIMAMOTO

THE FATHER

Kazuto Shimamoto studied with Kushida Kazuyoshi 1993–95 at Hon Free-Theatre School, and has performed at major houses throughout Japan including Theatre Cocoon, Tokyo, directors such as Takanori Kikuchi, Youko Narahashi and Yukio Ninagawa. He joined Shinjuku Ryozanpaku in 2012, performing in *Udagawa Twin-Suicide* by Kyouji Kobayashi 2012/13. In 2013/14 he performed and toured in FurukawaHideo's *Try Sleeping with a Hibernating Bear* directed by Yukio Ninagawa.

KEINA DENDA

THE DAUGHTER

Keina Denda is 26 years old. She majored in 'engeki' contemporary or underground theatre, at Touhoku Academy joined the company in 2008 for their tour to Brazil of *Great King Yebi* and since, has performed with the company continuously among many plays currently in repertory: *Shinagawa Love Suicide*, by Kyouji Kobayashi and *Bengal Tiger* by Juro Kara. For Shinjuku Ryozanpaku's all-female 'sister company', Project Nyx she performed in Terayama Shuji's *The Seven Deadly Sins of Princess Kikuko* directed by Kana Hiroshima. In 2013 she played Juliet.

REECE VELLA

THE SON

Reece Vella is 28 years old. He was born in Malta and has been in Australia for over six years. He originally came to Australia to study acting and has been pursuing his passion in theatre and on screen ever since. He is a graduate of Actors College of Theatre & TV, 2010 and has worked with director Lech Mackiewicz on *Ditto, A Love Story* (Sydney, Melbourne 2013), *Mixed Drink* (directed by Sean O'Riordan) and *OnLine* (directed by Celia Kelly). Since graduating in 2012 he has also worked in a variety of short films and television roles.

(From left) Lech Mackiewicz, Kathleen Doyle, Matt Crosby and Carly McGregor. (Photo: Kazuto Shimamoto)

Artists were asked:

What is it about the play?
What is it about the character?
What is it about the production that appeals to me?

Everyman – Maude Davey

The play is a slippery one, very very full, so I need to sit with it and think it through. This is the kind of full, rich ambitious text that I love the most. It's about something, but it doesn't reduce difficulty to aphorism. It's grand and takes the whole world as its stage – well, the western world. It's sort of like a summing up of the twentieth century and a prognosis for the twenty first. That's challenging. That's exciting. That's the kind of theatre we dream about being involved in.

So my challenge is to be as interesting as I can possibly be... as the trickster, the Harlequin, the MC. It's gonna take a lot of energy I think. Again, just the way I like it.

The biggest appeal is the team of amazing artists – with such diverse skills and experience. I am looking forward to being pushed beyond my own habits and comfortable routines into something more... that's what I want from my work now, to feel like I'm not pulling out the tricks that will work, but that I am finding new tricks, entering new worlds, opening up new possibilities for myself as an artist. That's what *Everyman* offers.

The Grandmother - Jane Bayly

Family dynamics, androgyny, impending apocalypse, the opportunity to work with this exciting group of artists and a dynamic dancing matriarch to play... yes please!

The Grandfather - Matt Crosby

The end of the world huh? The future exists only because of our past. - quite a past to have killed the future. Animals cry to block the pain that rings in their ear. And all we can do is dance.

The Mother - Kathleen Doyle

I play the role of the Mother in Everyman. The backdrop of the apocalypse prompts the Mother to question herself and her relationships frankly. 'I wanted my revenge on all men. I wanted to be a man.' These assertions originally struck me as those spoken from a woman who has become bitter or dissatisfied with her life and bored in her marriage. Then with further reflection it struck me that her words touch on the limitations we all feel with the immensity of our self in the narrow and confining roles we necessarily have to play in relation other people. Does the character of the Mother feel that she has lost 'herself' in her social roles of mother/wife/woman? I imagine that for the Mother, the spontaneity of dance offers the feeling of being alive and the experience of a more expansive sense of self. I am most interested in exploring how this discovery of the Mother connects to us all in some way.

The Father - Kazuto Shimamoto

I think I'm so lucky, very pleased to have been selected for the activities with Auto Da Fe.

Living in different country, also speaking different language, but I am very much looking forward to doing such a creative activity alongside senior experienced actors. I am also facing great anxiety at the same time. Because there is no image at all what happens. But, considerable work to seek in such anxiety and expectation that what I can contribute is the mission of me. Of course I do not forget that I myself enjoy this. Because I think the audience who look at it will really enjoy it.

The Daughter - Keina Denda

In a foreign country 'Australia', in a place to visit for the first time, and with the people who I will meet for the first time in my life, the experience of creating a play is a very big event for me! Thank you for give me the opportunity like this. In this play, the communication of each character unfolds comically, including the darkness of human history, rather than expressed in words, I think this play is to 'feel' and it works. As I play the role of 'daughter', I want to express that the feelings of 'I want to know!', such as in a pure question.

The Son - Reece Vela

The first time I read the play, I fell in love with the grandfather character. Now that I am playing grandson, I keep finding things I love about him and that I connect with. It's one interesting family.

I am highly intrigued about working with an international cast. Different cultures bring different points of view to a subject and sometimes surprisingly similar ideas. I like the melting pot and the collision of different backgrounds.

I am all about breaking down boundaries, asking relevant questions and exploring context and with this play and cast I am sure there will be plenty of this.

As I read the play over and over, I get initial ideas, then I let go of the play and forget about it. Sometimes new ideas come to me in this 'procrastinating moment'. My favourite part is rehearsals, when we get to play and explore together and bounce ideas off each other. I enjoy not having too much of a preconceived idea of what should be.

Art-installation design - Naomi Ota

For *Everyman & the Pole Dancers* I designed and created a theatrical installation which reflects memories of the past and presence in both Australia and Japan. The hybrid scenery suggests a world with multilayered stories. The elements are simple yet aesthetically detailed and show other dimensions when performers interact with them.

Light design - Shane Grant

This family is my family
This pole is my pole
This dance is my dance.

Composer - Noriko Tadano

This photo was taken In Japan when I was 6 years old. I started playing Shamisen when I was this age.

Each character in *Everyman* is vastly different. My challenge is to collaborate with each character to showcase their feelings through my Shamisen music.

Production Manager - Lara Week

I love the descriptions of each of the players, so precise and undefined at once. Writing like this puts itself into the hands of the cast and crew and says Here I am, what will you make of me?

Stage Manager - Carly McGregor

Carly is really excited to be part of this project, she is intrigued by the play and looks forward to seeing how it comes to life onstage.

THANK YOU

Majid Shokor

Nikki Shiels

Greg Ulfan

Emily Tomlins

Chris Uber

Kelvin Stevens

Sarah Woods

The White House, Sonya Fleming & James Berrell

Puma Media, Ted Matkowski

Kumai Masahiko

Big Fish Design, Alfons van Maanen and Renata Slusarski

Melbourne Anarchist Club, Ben, Dave, Angie and Brendan

Carrillo and Ziyin Gantner

Sheree Minehan

Shinko Miura

JICC, Keiko Egusa, Kumiko Toyama

Adam Hanuszkiewicz

Sarah Woods

Matylda Mackiewicz-Walton

Katherine Dodd

Above: Kazuto Shimamoto, Reece Vella and Carly McGregor. (Photo Matt Crosby)

Below: Jane Bayly. (Photo: Kazuto Shimamoto)

Above: Maude Davey. (Photo: Adam Hanuszkiewicz)

Below: Maude Davey, Keina Denda, Noriko Tadano, Naomi Ota, Kathleen Doyle, Reece Vella, Jane Bayly, Lech Mackiewicz. (Photo: Kazuto Shimamoto)